The Laughing Shepherd

by Angela Kecojevic
Illustrated by Erin Brown

OXFORD
UNIVERSITY PRESS

Chapter 1
Winter has arrived

Long, long ago …

Ivan pulled his red, woollen hat down over his ears, grabbed his sledge, and headed out into the snow. Winter had arrived in the Durmitor Mountains, and the sheep needed bringing home before darkness fell.

Even though it snowed every year, Ivan still gasped in amazement at the beautiful <u>scene</u> around him. Fir trees glimmered as though sprinkled with diamonds. Streams and rivers, once flowing with fish, were now frosted over with ice.

Close your eyes and picture the <u>scene</u> in front of Ivan. What else might he see? What might he hear and feel?

Just then, a whoosh of black and brown fur nearly knocked Ivan off his feet.

"Hey!" he cried. "Careful, Aria!"

Aria, the sheepdog, barked excitedly as they headed up the mountainside and snapped at snowflakes that fluttered against her nose.

Aria nearly knocked Ivan off his feet. Have you ever nearly had an accident, or nearly dropped something, but managed not to?

When Ivan was halfway up the mountain, he put a whistle to his lips and blew.

Peep. Peep. Peep.

Bells jingled in the distance. Ivan blew again.

Peep. Peep. Peep.

Soon, a flock of twelve sheep appeared over the mountainside.

"Go get them, Aria!" said Ivan.

When Aria had rounded up the sheep, Ivan jumped on his sledge and whizzed back down the mountain after his flock. Ivan grinned. The animals were part of his family. Nothing could ever replace them.

"Ya! Ya!" he whooped happily.

"Woof! Woof!" Aria barked.

"Baa! Baa!" the sheep bleated.

Do you have anything that you would not want to replace?

"It sounds like you're talking to one another," said Ivan's brother, who was holding open the barn door.

Ivan herded the sheep inside. "Not talking," he replied. "Laughing!"

"Laughing?" his brother said, <u>gently</u> closing the door. "Animals do not laugh!"

Ivan's brother closed the door <u>gently</u>. What would be the opposite of closing the door <u>gently</u>?

"They do," insisted Ivan. "They laugh when I tell them stories … especially the one about The Whispering Bear, who sat in a tree all day and night whispering to the bees to fetch him honey."

"Why would the bees do something so silly?" asked his brother.

"The bear tricked them," chuckled Ivan. "He told them he was the biggest, strongest, furriest bee they had ever seen!"

Ivan threw back his head and laughed until his belly ached. His brother began laughing, too.

"You always tell such funny stories, and you are always laughing," said his brother, wiping tears from his eyes. "You should be called The Laughing Shepherd!"

Chapter 2
Work, work, work

On the far side of the kingdom, Princess Sophia glanced unhappily out of the window. The sky was dark and angry, just like her father, the king.

A maid hurried over to the long wooden table where Sophia was sitting and put down a china bowl filled with beetroot soup. Sophia pushed it away.

"Are you not hungry, daughter?" demanded the king, from the other end of the table.

"No, Father," Sophia said quietly.

"You need to work up an appetite," the king boomed. "You must study harder!"

"But, Father," said Sophia with a sigh, "I already know why the mist settles over the valley in the morning, why the sun disappears each evening, and why the moon sparkles on the lake."

If you demand something, you ask for it very strongly. Can you read the king's question again, as if you were demanding an answer?

"That is not enough!" said the king, spluttering on his beetroot soup. "One day you must rule this precious kingdom. The people will expect you to know *everything*!"

"I study all day long!" sobbed Sophia. "What I really want is to be able to play and laugh like the other children."

"Play?" the king boomed, his face turning as purple as his soup. "Laugh?"

Something that is precious is worth a lot or is very special. What is precious to you?

The king was so angry that he sent Sophia to her room.

"Work, work, work," she said crossly, kicking off her silver slippers. "That's all Father wants me to do." She sat down heavily on her bed. "I shall not leave my room until someone makes me laugh!"

Chapter 3
Chaos!

A month passed, and Sophia stayed true to her word. She didn't leave her room once.

"What can I do?" the king grumbled, as he paced up and down the grand library. "I only wish for Sophia to be happy. Perhaps I have been too harsh."

He summoned the royal jester. He summoned the royal puppeteer. He even summoned the royal acrobat. Sophia did not laugh once.

It was on the morning of Sophia's eleventh birthday that something unusual happened. She was standing by her window, looking out across the great frozen lake, when she saw a flock of sheep. The sheep were wearing silver bells that made the prettiest sound Sophia had ever heard. A shepherd boy, with a red, woollen hat, was pulling a sledge. A sheepdog was sitting on the sledge.

"Ya! Ya!" the boy shouted.

"Woof! Woof!" the sheepdog barked.

"Baa! Baa!" the sheep bleated.

Laughter bubbled in Sophia's throat. "It sounds as though they are talking to each other!"

Ivan had trekked over the mountain, skidded over streams, and sledged across the ice to reach the king's palace. Like everyone in the kingdom, he had heard of Sophia's sadness. He hoped he could be the one to make her laugh again.

He knocked on the palace door and was greeted by a butler with a beard so long that it almost tickled the floor.

Suddenly, before Ivan could stop them, the animals raced past the butler and into the palace. The butler gasped. The maid gasped. Even the king, who was reading in his library, gasped.

Never before had they seen such a sight!

Ivan chased the animals through the kitchen, across the dining hall, and then up a wide staircase. The <u>scene</u> was chaos!

"Stop! Stop!" Ivan cried.

"Woof! Woof!" Aria barked.

"Baa! Baa!" the sheep bleated.

Picture the <u>scene</u> in your head. What might have happened as the animals ran through the kitchen and across the dining hall?

It was only the sound of gentle laughter that finally made the animals stop.

Sophia was standing in the doorway of her bedroom, her cheeks as pink as a spring rose.

"Thank you," she said softly. "I cannot remember when I last laughed so much!"

Who was laughing gently? Can you give a gentle laugh?

Ivan felt happier than ever. "Would you like to hear the story of The Whispering Bear?"

"I would like that very much," replied Sophia.

Sophia and Ivan went downstairs and sat near the fire. The maid fetched warm cinnamon cakes and hot berry tea, and, as the sun slipped behind the mountain, Ivan began his story.

When he had finished, Sophia began to laugh … and laugh … and laugh.

"What a clever bear!" she exclaimed. "What silly bees!"

Everyone was overjoyed to see Sophia smiling again, especially the king.

"I <u>demand</u> that you come and see us every week, Ivan!" the king said.

Ivan smiled and promised he would.

The king <u>demands</u> that Ivan comes back every week. How is <u>demanding</u> different from asking?

People travelled from far and wide to hear Ivan's precious stories. Every Sunday the sound of bells rang out over the mountainside as Ivan, Aria and the sheep made their way to the palace. They would sit on the great lawn and, when everyone was ready, Ivan would begin:

"Long, long ago …"

Lots of people wanted to hear Ivan's precious stories. Do you have any stories that are special to you?

The Whispering Bear

Have a go at making up your own story about The Whispering Bear. Try to use the following words to help tell your story: demand, gentle, nearly, precious, replace, scene.